I HAVE NOT YET BEGUN TO FIGHT

A Creative Minds Biography

I HAVE NOT YET BEGUN TO FIGHT

A Story about John Paul Jones

by Elaine Marie Alphin and
Arthur B. Alphin

illustrations by Paul Casale

Carolrhoda Books, Inc./Minneapolis

*To all the American sailors whose lives have been
lost at sea in the defense of freedom and whose
souls eternally stand at their post, at the bottom
of the ocean*   —E. M. A. and A. B. A.

Text copyright © 2004 by Elaine Marie Alphin and Arthur B. Alphin
Illustrations copyright © 2004 by Paul Casale

This book is available in two editions:
Library binding by Carolrhoda Books, Inc.,
    a division of Lerner Publishing Group
Soft cover by First Avenue Editions,
    an imprint of Lerner Publishing Group
241 First Avenue North
Minneapolis, MN 55401 U.S.A.

Website address: www.lernerbooks.com

Library of Congress Cataloging-in-Publication-Data

Alphin, Elaine Marie.
    I have not yet begun to fight : a story about John Paul Jones / by Elaine
Marie Alphin and Arthur B. Alphin ; illustrations by Paul Casale.
        p.   cm. — (A creative minds biography)
    Summary: Describes the life of John Paul Jones, who served in
America's navy during the Revolutionary War and is remembered for
saying, "I have not yet begun to fight." Includes bibliographical references
and index.
    ISBN: 1–57505–601–1 (lib. bdg. : alk. paper)
    ISBN: 1–57505–635–6 (phk · alk. paper)
    1. Jones, John Paul, 1747–1792—Juvenile literature. 2. Admirals—
United States—Biography—Juvenile literature. 3. United States. Navy—
Biography—Juvenile literature. 4. United States—History—Revolution,
1775–1783—Naval operations—Juvenile literature. [1. Jones, John Paul,
1747–1792. 2. Admirals. 3. United States. Navy—Biography. 4. United
States—History—Revolution, 1775–1783—Naval operations.] I. Alphin,
Arthur B. II. Casale, Paul, ill. III. Title. IV. Series.
E207.J7A78 2004
973.3'5'092—dc22   2003012117

Manufactured in the United States of America
1 2 3 4 5 6 – JR – 09 08 07 06 05 04

Table of Contents

To Go to Sea   7

Accused of Murder   16

The Sea War for Liberty   25

Outsmarting the British Navy   35

"In Pursuit of Honor"   43

"I Have Not Yet Begun to Fight"   50

Afterword: Universal Esteem   57

Seafaring Terms   60

Selected Bibliography   61

Index   62

About the Authors and Illustrator   64

1

To Go to Sea

John Paul stood on a low cliff overlooking the River Nith, near his home in Scotland. Below him, a group of boys sat ready in rowboats and small sailboats, looking up at their young admiral. The boys had been talking about Great Britain's war with France. (Scotland, along with England and other lands, was part of the vast British Empire.) In 1757 British warships won nearly all their sea battles. But ten-year-old John Paul was sure he could command those warships even better than the famous British admirals.

In his thick Scottish accent, John shouted the order to advance. One fleet of sailboats pushed off. Shading his hazel eyes against the sun, John motioned the other boats to circle around. This second group moved into position to attack. For a few moments, John forgot that he was a barefoot boy whose chestnut hair blew in a country breeze instead of the ocean's salty winds. He felt the glory of command as sailors listened and obeyed him.

But then the boys erupted in laugher, splashing each other with paddles. John shouted angrily, but they ignored him. They couldn't see the larger picture that John saw from the cliff. Even though he was only looking at sailboats, John imagined a naval fleet spread out beneath him. He saw just how he could direct the battle so his ships would win. It wasn't a game to John, as it was to the others.

Furious and hurt, he ran home across rolling green fields dotted with white hawthorn blossoms. The Pauls' three-room cottage felt crowded with his mother, his older sisters, Elizabeth and Janet, and his little sister, Mary Ann. But John shut them out and lost himself in his schoolbooks.

The Reverend James Hogg, who taught the church school, gave his students plenty of lessons in Latin, French, math, and English. As John read about distant lands, he dreamed of sailing down the River Nith, past the bay of Solway Firth that separated Scotland from England, all the way to the ocean. He hoped that education and hard work could transform him from a boy playing admiral into a man that sailors and sea captains would respect.

John's father, John Paul Senior, designed and tended elegant flower gardens on a large estate called Arbigland. John's mother worked as a housekeeper for

Mr. Craik, the estate owner. When she married John Senior, Mr. Craik built a comfortable white stone cottage for the Paul family. The couple had high hopes for their children, even though they didn't have much money. They saved what they could to give their daughters enough money to marry. That didn't leave much money to give John and his older brother, William, but the Pauls encouraged the boys to choose work they would enjoy doing.

John couldn't imagine spending his life growing flowers. His father was well liked, but he wasn't an important man whom other men looked up to. William had gone across the Atlantic Ocean to the American colonies when John was nine. He'd opened a tailor's shop in Virginia. William's letters urged his brother to join him, but John couldn't see how a shop-keeper could make any greater mark on the world than a gardener. John believed his future lay on the high seas.

As often as he could slip away, John walked to the Carselthorn port. He explored the ships docked there and questioned the seamen eagerly. The sailors told him about their adventures and taught him words in strange languages from faraway places. Some even showed him some seamanship basics, like knot tying. They were surprised at how quickly he learned.

When John was thirteen, he left school to go to sea. He thought about joining the British navy. Wealthy families paid a fee so their sons could train to become British naval officers. John knew his father couldn't afford to pay a fee. But his visits with the seamen gave him another idea. Perhaps he could join the crew of a trading ship. He'd apprentice himself to a shipping company, promising to work for them for a certain number of years in exchange for learning how to be a sailor.

John's father found an English shipowner named John Younger who was looking for a new apprentice. The Pauls sent their son off with their blessings, and Mr. Craik gave him a gold sovereign to help buy the things he would need for his new work. John sailed to Whitehaven, England, and convinced Mr. Younger to hire him.

John and Mr. Younger signed an agreement in 1761. John would work for Younger's Shipping Company for seven years. He would begin as ship's boy on Younger's brig, *Friendship*.

Unlike larger ships with three masts, brigs had two masts, with wide, horizontal sails. John soon discovered how much the sailors in Carselthorn had helped him by teaching him his ship's knots. One of his first jobs involved tying knots high up in the rigging.

This arrangement of ropes supported the masts and raised, lowered, and adjusted the ship's sails. John could tie the ropes quickly and securely, and then untie them again, even in high winds or cold rains. His ability impressed the *Friendship's* master, Robert Benson. But that didn't mean he spoiled John!

If John thought his family's stone cottage was crowded, he learned what crowded really meant when he settled into life on a ship at sea. Mr. Benson and his officers had small, private cabins. But the rest of the twenty-eight-man crew slept packed together in a cramped, dark room below the decks. As the most junior crew member, John probably hung his hammock in the darkest corner. When the wake-up call sounded, sailors had to roll up their hammocks because the night's bedroom quickly became the day's workroom.

John spent most of his time scrubbing decks, hauling buckets of water for other seamen or the ship's cook, weaving the ends of broken ropes together, mending sails, cleaning equipment, lugging gunpowder and shot for the brig's guns, carrying messages— whatever he was told. John and the crew on deck could only see the small work area around them. Officers stood above watching, the way John had watched the boys sailing on the River Nith. They saw the larger picture, and when they shouted an order, it was important for sailors to obey instantly.

If a sailor hesitated, it could mean serious injury or damage to the ship if a sail swung loose. Because of these dangers, punishment for disobedience was swift, painful, and public. The petty officer in charge of the sailors on deck carried a knotted rope to lash anyone who didn't move fast enough. Repeat offenders or seamen who talked back might be flogged in front of the whole crew with the cat-o'-nine-tails— nine knotted ropes bound together into one whip.

Hesitation in battle could mean death. Britain was fighting France in what would later be called the Seven Years' War. Both nations wanted to rule trade on the high seas and to control the growing colonies in North America. Even trading ships like the *Friendship* had to be ready to fight if they met a French vessel.

Despite the war, the *Friendship* had a peaceful voyage across the Atlantic Ocean to Barbados, an island in the West Indies. John learned to obey orders without question. And as he carried messages to the upper decks or climbed the rigging, he learned to look at the larger picture as an officer would. He was determined that someday he would be the officer issuing the orders.

Barbados was the first exotic country John had seen, after hearing so many sailors' yarns for years. He thought the stop to load a cargo of rum and sugar was interesting, but not as exciting as mastering a seaman's skills. And Barbados was less inviting than their next stop: Virginia. John was eager to see his brother, William.

William's tailor shop was doing very well. He welcomed his brother and proudly introduced John to his friends, reminding everyone they were Scottish, not English. Scotland and England might both be part of Great Britain, but it was England's government and king that made most laws. The Scottish disliked the English telling them how to run their country.

In 1761 many American colonists were also frustrated by England's harsh treatment. John had read William's letters protesting the unfair taxes and the English government's refusal to listen to colonial complaints. Here he saw and heard the people's anger for himself.

John also saw how beautiful Virginia was. Although he wanted a career at sea, he decided to buy land and settle there one day. He later wrote this was "my favorite country from the age of thirteen when first I saw it." Delighted that his brother loved Virginia, William presented John to friends who could help him, like George Washington's sister and her husband.

Visiting these important families, John realized that America was a place where achievement and character earned respect. The class a person was born into wasn't as important as it was in Britain. If John worked hard and succeeded at sea, and behaved like a gentleman on land, then important people in America would respect him even though his father was only a gardener. But John also noticed that William's friends spoke proper English and dressed like gentlemen. He vowed to lose his Scottish accent and earn enough money to dress well himself.

After the *Friendship* returned to Whitehaven, John spent Christmas with his family. During the next three years, he sailed regularly between England, Barbados, and the colonies. Between voyages, he improved his speaking and writing skills. He also studied navigation to learn how to figure out a ship's position at sea and chart its course.

Then, in 1764, Younger's Shipping Company went out of business. Seventeen-year-old John found his apprenticeship unexpectedly over. John had learned a great deal sailing on the *Friendship*, but now he had to look for new ways to prove his merit at sea.

2

Accused of Murder

John became third mate on the *King George*. This ship carried captured Africans from the coast of West Africa to the West Indies. There, traders sold the Africans as slaves. The ship's conditions were miserable, with the prisoners packed in tightly and treated like animals. John hated the work, but the pay was good. John could save money for the Virginia land he planned to buy.

After two years aboard the *King George,* John signed on the *Two Friends* as chief mate. This ship sailed from Kingston, Jamaica, to West Africa, carrying rum and supplies. It then returned with its cargo holds crammed with imprisoned Africans. As chief mate, John had greater responsibility and earned more money. But he couldn't stand the way the Africans were mistreated. He said the slave trade was "abominable," or too awful to be described. He refused to make another voyage on the *Two Friends.*

Perhaps John sympathized with the Africans' loss of their homes and families even more because he had just lost his father. John had the tombstone engraved: "In Memory of John Paul Senior who died at Arbigland the 24 October 1767. Universally esteemed. Erected by John Paul Junior." John honored his father with the tribute he himself most wanted, universal esteem. In the 1700s, esteem was high praise. It meant that important people valued and respected you for yourself and for your accomplishments. John was sure he could earn that esteem by better means than carrying people to be sold.

In Kingston, John met Samuel McAdam, a fellow Scotsman. McAdam was master of a brig that was about to sail for England. He offered John free passage home in exchange for help on the ship. It must have seemed like fate to John, because the brig was named the *John.*

On the voyage, both McAdam and his first mate caught a fever and died. None of the remaining sailors knew how to navigate. Twenty-one-year-old John saw his chance to prove himself. Although he wasn't even an officer, John took command. The time he'd spent studying navigation and the experience he'd gotten on other ships paid off. He sailed the *John* safely home.

Relieved to see their brig and cargo, the owners named John Paul master of the *John*. During the next two years, John circled between America, the West Indies, and England. On one voyage, he even sailed home from Kingston in record time. John did so well because he made his crew follow strict rules. He expected them to work as hard and as well as he did. At first, the sailors resented this rigid discipline. Then they saw how smoothly the brig sailed under his command, even in sudden storms. When he gave an order, they obeyed without complaint.

In 1769 the *John*'s owners hired a new ship's carpenter, Mungo Maxwell. Mungo wasn't used to such a demanding master. He did poor work on the voyage to Barbados and was slow to obey John's orders. Seeing this, other sailors slacked off. John lost his temper, as he had when the boys on the River Nith wouldn't listen to him. But he was no longer a boy. He was a seasoned ship's master who was used to instant obedience. He ordered Mungo flogged with the cat-o'-nine-tails. His crew grew obedient again.

When they docked in the West Indies island of Tobago, Mungo went to court. He complained that John had mistreated him, and he showed the judge his scars from the cat-o'-nine-tails as evidence. But the judge had seen disobedient sailors flogged before.

He threw out Mungo's complaint.

Neither John nor Mungo wanted to sail home on the same ship. Mungo took passage on the *Barcelona Packet*—but onboard he caught a fever and died. When Mungo's father heard, he insisted that the flogging, not the fever, had caused his son's death. John was arrested for murder when he landed in Kircudbright, Scotland.

Outraged, John insisted that Mungo hadn't died because of the flogging. He promised to give the court proof if the judge let him return to the West Indies. The judge agreed.

People in Kircudbright felt sorry for Mungo's father. But they didn't all blame John. In November 1770, the men of the Kircudbright Masonic lodge welcomed John into the brotherhood of Freemasons. The brotherhood was an international organization of professional men, wealthy men, and even royalty. Freemasons pledged themselves to God and to each other. They held meetings where they carried out sacred, secret rituals. They also pledged to support their brothers in everything any one of them attempted. John knew that many of William's friends in America were Freemasons. As a brother mason, perhaps he could win the esteem he longed for.

John returned from the West Indies in 1772. He

brought a sworn statement from the judge in Tobago, explaining the facts of Mungo's case. John also presented a statement from the *Barcelona Packet*'s captain. The man swore that Mungo had been healthy when he left Tobago. The captain also said that Mungo had caught a fever during the voyage and died at sea. The Kirkcudbright judge weighed the evidence and cleared John of all charges.

But some people still believed he was guilty of murder. John quickly sent a letter to his mother. He asked her to tell Mr. Craik, the estate owner who had helped his family so much, that the judge had cleared him in Mungo's death. John wanted to be sure that men who had thought well of him continued to do so.

John returned his attention to his goals. He had already used some of his profits to buy land in America. He also bought part ownership of a ship called the *Betsy* in 1772. She carried cargo between England and Ireland and the West Indies islands of Madeira and Tobago.

In less than two years, John made a small fortune— nearly twenty-five hundred pounds. His good record and his determination impressed the men whose esteem he intended to earn. So did his neat appearance. John dressed more like a naval officer than a merchant ship's master, even wearing a sword.

But John's strict discipline and hot temper didn't always please his crew. The *Betsy* sailed into Tobago in 1773 after a long, hard voyage. The ship had sprung a leak and been delayed six months for repairs in Ireland. Then John came down with a fever. Many of the crew were local Tobago men who felt they'd earned some fun. They demanded their pay immediately, even though their contract said they'd be paid after the cargo was sold. John refused. They'd get their money as agreed, not sooner.

One angry seaman, whom John called the Ringleader, stole a boat to take his friends ashore without permission. John tried to stop him. But the Ringleader attacked John, forcing him back into his cabin. Enraged, John seized his sword and charged out on deck. He planned to frighten the Ringleader, but the man was much larger—John stood only five feet, five inches. The Ringleader leaped out of the boat he was stealing, grabbed a heavy stick, and attacked John. This was mutiny!

John backed away, ordering the man to stop. But the Ringleader pressed forward. Standing at the edge of the deck beneath the man's upraised stick, John ran the mutineer through with his sword.

Not waiting for anyone to charge him with murder, John immediately went ashore and turned himself in.

The justice of the peace told him he was free until the court could hear his case. However, John's friends advised him to change his name and flee rather than wait to stand to trial. They feared the locals might attack him. And a jury might sympathize more with a dead local seaman than a foreign captain who had once before faced murder charges.

John knew he hadn't committed murder—he'd killed a mutineer in self-defense. But he reluctantly decided to listen to his friends. He didn't even take time to recover his money and belongings. He fled with only what he had in his pockets and what his friends could give him.

John Paul never stood trial for murder in Tobago. Instead, a young man who called himself John Paul Jones appeared in Virginia at his brother's tailor shop—only to learn that William had died. At twenty-six, John found himself alone in a new country with a new name and very little money. But he still had his old determination to earn men's esteem, and he had the seafaring skills he'd worked so hard to master. These skills were exactly what he would need in his new home. America was about to do battle with Britain's powerful navy.

3

The Sea War for Liberty

By the time John arrived in Virginia in 1774, the American colonies had moved closer to war with Britain. Many people were angrier than ever about unfair taxes and laws. At the First Continental Congress, representatives from most of the colonies talked about ways to gain more rights from Britain.

John thought that the American colonies should stand up for their rights and declare their independence. But he wasn't sure how he could help the cause of liberty. His experience had been in peaceful trading. John began to study naval warfare. He brought to this task the same determination with which he'd earlier studied navigation—and the same intensity with which he'd once played admiral.

Freemason friends introduced John to other supporters of liberty. He met Joseph Hewes and Thomas Jefferson, delegates to the Continental Congress, and Patrick Henry. For a short time, John and Patrick Henry courted the same girl, Dorothea Dandridge. John hoped that marriage to her would earn him the esteem he so longed for. But Dorothea's father decided that Henry would make a better son-in-law. He turned down John's marriage proposal.

John didn't have time to be heartbroken. The fight for American liberty distracted him. In April 1775, British soldiers and American colonists fired on each other in Massachusetts. The Revolutionary War had begun, even though Congress hadn't yet declared independence. George Washington began forming the Continental army and urged Congress to establish a navy as well. John decided he might earn esteem by fighting at sea instead of simply marrying well.

Control of the seas was important. The colonists couldn't grow or make all the supplies people used, so they needed items from Europe. If British warships blocked American harbors, they could stop supplies from getting through. That would make it harder for America to win a war. The colonies needed a

Continental navy to fight the British navy—but they had no warships.

Building warships from scratch was expensive and could take up to a year. Congress had neither money nor time. Instead they bought four merchant ships to convert into warships. Next Congress looked for sea captains. John asked Joseph Hewes to recommend him, promising that his "friendship and good opinion [would not be] misplaced." On December 7, 1775, Congress made John a first lieutenant in the Continental navy.

His first assignment was to take temporary command of the *Alfred* in Philadelphia. Her permanent commander, Captain Dudley Saltonstall, would arrive later. What training should John give the *Alfred*'s crew to prepare them for war?

Studying naval history had taught John that the British won their sea battles with rapid fire. John drilled his crew to load and shoot and reload the ship's cannon. Soon the men could quickly load the guns with black powder and cannonballs. They could open the gun ports, use ropes to haul the guns into position, and then fire them, never making a mistake. Once they could follow the drill perfectly under John's demanding watch, he knew they would be able to do their job under fire at sea as professionally as any experienced British sailor.

John took pride in his well-drilled seamen. But his proudest duty before he turned over command of the *Alfred* was to fly the brand new Grand Union Flag. This flag's thirteen red and white stripes stood for the thirteen colonies. The crosses of Saint Andrew and Saint George stood for John's Scotland and America's mother country, England. John wrote, "I hoisted [raised] with my own hands, the Flag of Freedom the first time it was displayed."

Then Captain Saltonstall, a seaman from an important New England family, arrived to take over. He was pleased with the preparation John had given his seamen, and instructed Lieutenant Jones to continue the training program.

In April 1776, the navy's commander, Commodore Eset Hopkins, led his tiny fleet to the Bahamas. He successfully seized the ammunition and supplies the British had stored there. But two days later, a British warship, the HMS *Glasgow,* attacked them. John knew that the *Alfred* was only a converted merchant ship and could not move or turn as quickly as a warship. This put the *Alfred* in great danger from the *Glasgow.*

British warships always tried to get in position to fire all of their guns on one side at the enemy vessel.

This was called a broadside. But merchant ships were built differently than warships. They were built to carry cargo, not to support the weight of guns. Their design made them slower and harder to steer than warships. And their thinner walls meant that enemy fire could do serious damage. The *Glasgow*'s guns fired devastating broadsides, damaging the *Alfred* so badly that the crew couldn't steer. Captain Saltonstall withdrew for repairs.

John didn't think the *Alfred* should have retreated, even if the ship was unsuitable for war. He thought that a captain should figure out how to get the best performance out of the ship he had been given. Since John had been in command of the *Alfred,* however briefly, he was also afraid he might be blamed for the retreat. But his training program must have impressed Commodore Hopkins. When the American fleet returned to Philadelphia, the commodore made John temporary captain of the *Providence,* a fast, one-masted ship called a sloop.

John immediately got to work drilling his new crew of seventy men. He wanted them at least as well trained as the *Alfred*'s crew. A sloop was easier to steer than a converted merchant ship. But it wasn't large enough to face a British warship in battle. John kept wondering how he could make up for the weaknesses of American ships and turn them into strengths.

On August 6, the Continental navy gave John orders to "seize, take, sink, burn or destroy [the ships] of our enemies." Two days later, he was made a captain. John should have been overjoyed, but he wasn't. Some of the navy's other captains had the backing of powerful friends. Others, like Captain Saltonstall, came from old colonial families. These men had become captains before John. That meant they would receive command assignments sooner than John, and they would also get better ships.

In reality, John was lucky to be promoted to captain at all. He was a self-made man with an invented name. But it frustrated him that he was still not as highly esteemed as other men. He made up his mind to prove his worth to the Navy with the *Providence.* On the sloop's first solo cruise, John captured the *Britannia,* a British whaling ship. He sent some of his crewmen to sail the ship back to Philadelphia as a prize of war. He also convinced some of the *Britannia's* men to enlist in the Continental navy and join his crew.

During the second half of August, the *Providence* crisscrossed the Atlantic Ocean, chasing and attacking British warships. One of John's greatest qualities was his ability to come up with unusual new solutions to problems. He wasn't afraid to try unconventional ideas that no one else had thought of before. His sloop might carry fewer guns than British warships, but his crew followed orders so well that he could zigzag faster than well-trained British seamen. He chased the HMS *Solebay* around the island of Bermuda, using speed and clever sailing to outrun the big English frigate.

In September John captured other ships, including the *Sea Nymph*. He sent the vessel with its cargo of rum, sugar, ginger, oil, and wine to Philadelphia. In light of his success, he asked Congress to make him equal to the navy's other captains. Congress was delighted with the prize cargo, but they didn't agree to John's request.

Next John put into port in Nova Scotia, Canada, for fresh food and supplies. There he saw a British frigate. The *Providence* couldn't possibly win a battle against a well-armed frigate, but John darted in and backed off, daring the captain to waste ammunition by firing when the *Providence* was too far away to be hit. The British captain finally fired all his cannons, even though the *Providence* was out of range. John responded with a single musket shot, mocking the captain for his foolishness.

John went on to capture the *Alexander,* the *Kingston Packet,* the *Success,* and the *Portland* before returning to America with his prizes in October. He'd seen several ways that unconventional thinking could give the American navy an edge over British warships. Could he convince other captains to try his ideas?

4

Outsmarting
the British Navy

John shared his schemes with Congress. He recommended an official training program for both officers and crew. That would mean that everyone would
practice the same exercises. All officers would call
out the same orders, and all seamen would react the
same way.

He also suggested new, smarter dress uniforms for
officers. These would give the navy increased
pride—and help fool the enemy. The dark blue coats
had white linings, with gold decorations on padded
shoulders. They looked very much like British naval
uniforms. American ships could sail quite close to

British ships before the British officers realized they were enemy ships.

Getting closer allowed smaller American vessels to swing beside the larger warships and lock the two vessels together with grappling irons. This was another unconventional way John had thought of to turn the weakness of American ships into battle strengths. When two ships were grappled side by side, the British warships didn't have enough space to fire their cannons properly.

To fire a cannon, British crews pushed the cannon's muzzle through a gun port and all the way outside the ship's wall. This way, smoke from the explosion escaped outside the ship. If a cannon was shot from inside the ship, smoke filled the gun deck and choked the crew. The noise was also deafening.

Reloading was difficult because space on the gun deck was tight. Men used a long, wooden tool called a ramrod to ram the gunpowder and ball into a cannon's muzzle. First they rolled the cannon back inside. Then they had to stick the ramrod outside the ship to load.

But when two ships were locked together by grappling irons, their sides pressed against each other. The seamen couldn't run the cannons out to shoot them. And they couldn't stretch their ramrods outside to reload. Grappling would silence some cannons, but warships also mounted cannons on their top decks. John had some unconventional ideas about those guns too.

He knew that the British navy trusted its fearsome cannon power to defeat enemy ships. Because of this, officers rarely gave crewmen pistols or muskets. John had spent long hours climbing the rigging. He knew what a clear view it gave of the deck below—or of the deck of a ship grappled alongside. He suggested putting men in the rigging with muskets. Then they could shoot the seamen on the top deck of the enemy ship, silencing the upper guns. By throwing grenades to start deck fires, these men might also damage the ship or destroy its guns.

Congress didn't approve all of John's ideas. They didn't start a training program. They said the new uniforms looked nice, but didn't insist that officers wear them, although many did. But they gave John command of the *Alfred.* (Captain Saltonstall was assigned to a different ship.) And they told John he could raid the Atlantic as he saw fit, trying out his new ideas. John chased several ships before capturing the *Active.* Then he defeated the HMS *Mellish,* a 350-ton armed transport. By late November, John had also captured three colliers (ships that carried coal) and a ten-gun merchant vessel, the *John.*

He formed the ships into a small fleet and was sailing toward Boston when he saw the HMS *Milford,* a British frigate armed with twenty-eight guns. John knew the *Milford*'s captain had seen him too. If the British realized he was American, the *Alfred* and the captured ships would be in great danger. So he signaled to the *Milford* as if he were another British ship, hoping to fool the crew. Just in case the trick didn't work, John arranged his captured ships to support him if he were forced into battle.

The dawn light revealed that the *Alfred* was American. The *Milford* attacked. John directed his ships like a little fleet, bringing the *Alfred* in position to fire broadside on the *Milford.* He succeeded in out-running the slower frigate and saving the *Mellish,* the *Active,* and the two colliers, but only by letting the British capture the *John.*

The *Mellish* was the big prize, however, as it carried supplies and winter uniforms. Thanks to John, some of those supplies reached George Washington's men before the bitterly cold Battle of Trenton. "The loss of the *Mellish* will distress the enemy more than can be easily imagined," wrote John.

His loss of the *John* troubled him. But Congress was impressed with his other successes and gave him command of the sloop *Ranger.* John wasn't satisfied.

During the first months of the war, Congress had placed orders for new frigates to lead the American fleet. John complained that he had only been given a sloop instead of one of the new frigates. He repeated his old complaint about rank too. John was only number eighteen out of twenty-four captains in the navy. Less capable officers got more important commands—like the new frigates—because they had become captains first.

Some congressmen privately agreed that John was a better captain than many of the others. John Hancock wrote to Robert Morris, "I admire the spirited conduct of little Jones; pray push him out again. I know he does not love to be idle." But the list remained unchanged, and in June 1777, John took command of the *Ranger.*

John was dissatisfied with the way his new ship was outfitted. The sails were poor quality, the crew couldn't hear the cheap whistles, and there wasn't enough fresh meat to feed his men. John spent his own money to buy supplies, live chickens, and clothes for his crew. The men never knew that John paid for these things from own pocket.

It would have surprised them, because John was never popular among his crews. He was too strict, and he rarely praised his men. He believed that a naval officer should be an absolute ruler aboard his ship but should also be absolutely fair in punishing or rewarding his men. John thought it was fair for his men to have fresh meat and proper clothes, even if he had to pay for them himself.

Before the *Ranger* sailed on November 1, news came that British General John Burgoyne had surrendered at Saratoga, New York, in October. John was ordered to carry this important information to Benjamin Franklin in France. Franklin was negotiating with King Louis XVI to get French money, supplies, and soldiers to support the war.

John knew that the news of the British surrender could help Franklin convince the king to support the colonies. Franklin was as pleased to meet John as he was to get the news. He admired the stubborn sailor and became one of John's strongest supporters.

During the winter, John sailed the *Ranger* along the French coast. One day he met a French squadron. John saw an opportunity to be shown the esteem he longed for. When ships commanded by officers of equal rank met, they fired an equal number of guns into the air as a salute. John sent a note to the squadron's admiral, asking to exchange thirteen-gun salutes.

But the French admiral knew that he outranked the

brash young captain. He replied that John could present a thirteen-gun salute, but he would respond with only a nine-gun salute. It wasn't what John felt he deserved, but he accepted. At least this was the first time the American flag had been saluted at sea.

That winter John also made new plans to attack the British navy. British ships had already attacked American coastal towns, burning homes. But no navy had attacked a British seaport since 1667. If American ships could successfully attack British ports, British warships would have to leave American towns alone and return to defend their own seacoast. It would be risky, but risk never stopped John.

Although John was only twenty-nine, Congress agreed to let him try. On April 10, 1778, John sailed the *Ranger* north on a daring raid. He was about to take the war to the enemy's doorstep.

5

"In Pursuit of Honor"

As his target, John chose Whitehaven, England. It was the port from which young John Paul had sailed aboard the *Friendship* seventeen years earlier. John left the *Ranger* at anchor and rowed into Whitehaven at midnight, dividing his men to attack separate points. He planned to set fire to the ships in port. He would also disable the harbor guns, leaving them useless.

John's men weren't enthusiastic about the raid. When they captured a ship at sea, they got a share of the prize money. The navy paid this money, based on the value of the captured goods. But this raid wouldn't bring them any prizes. Once ashore, some sailors stopped at a pub to discuss ways to find profit in Whitehaven. Another seaman actually disapproved of the Revolutionary War. He'd joined the *Ranger*'s crew hoping to get home. Wanting the raid to fail, he ran from house to house, shouting that the town was being invaded.

Hearing the shouts, armed townspeople ran outdoors to see what was happening. John's group had only disabled one group of harbor guns, and he refused to withdraw. He posted guards and set fire to a ship docked in the harbor. Then he led his two boat crews back to the *Ranger*.

Although the raid didn't do much damage, John had successfully attacked a British city. This showed the British navy that an American vessel could sail into one of their ports, enter the town, and escape without punishment.

John had another goal in mind when he attacked Whitehaven. He knew that British warships usually sailed in large fleets of twenty or more ships. So many ships could easily overwhelm one smaller ship like the *Ranger*. He needed to force the British navy to scatter their fleets. Then smaller American ships could attack a single British vessel and stand a good chance of defeating it.

If the British didn't know where an American attack might happen next, they would have to scatter their fleets to protect as many different potential targets as possible. So John kept attacking different ports. He sailed the *Ranger* across Solway Firth to Saint Mary's Isle, near his old home in Scotland. John planned to kidnap the Earl of Selkirk, a wealthy nobleman, and hold him for ransom.

Unfortunately, the earl wasn't there. John's crew wanted to seize everything they could carry and burn the house. John allowed them to take the family silver, but he ordered them not to harm the family or servants. John paid his crew the value of the silver— from his own pocket, without telling anyone. He returned the silver when the war ended.

After these two raids, John attacked the HMS *Drake*. He closed within pistol range quickly. The two ships battled for over an hour as dusk approached. To prevent the *Drake* from moving freely, John ordered his gunners to shoot the masts and sails. Finally the *Drake*'s captain and lieutenant were both killed.

The frigate was so badly crippled that John had to tow it back to France. The British navy tried to catch him, sending five frigates searching in different directions. As John had hoped, the navy was already scattering its force. He arrived safely in France with prizes and the news that the British navy no longer ruled the seas.

John hoped that Congress would reward his successes with a promotion. When Congress ordered the *Ranger* to return, John sent the sloop back. He stayed in France, hoping to be given command of a fleet. But to his disappointment, Congress didn't offer him that command.

John kept sending letters to his friends in America, pleading for a fleet. With Benjamin Franklin's support, John also sent letters to the French minister of war and to the French king and queen. John promised to sail "in harm's way," keeping the British navy tied up searching for him. He kept up his steady stream of letters until the king agreed to buy a merchant ship called the *Duc de Duras,* refit her as a man-of-war, and give her to John as his fleet command vessel.

Even though it was another converted merchant ship instead of a warship, John was grateful for this opportunity. He thanked Franklin for his help by renaming the ship in his honor. *Poor Richard's Almanack* was one of Franklin's most famous works. In French the title translated into *Les Maximes du Bonhomme Richard,* so John named his new ship the *Bonhomme Richard.*

John set to work outfitting the ship for war. He bought the best guns he could afford: some new, small cannons and six worn-out but larger cannons. The large guns could shoot heavy, eighteen-pound cannonballs that could smash through the walls of a sturdy British warship. He also bought four times as many muskets as a warship normally carried.

John recruited a crew of French sailors and enthusiastic volunteers. He asked for "none but volunteers who with all their hearts are determined to go with me anywhere and everywhere in pursuit of honor." He began training his men in gun drills, grappling, and fighting from the rigging.

John continued to ask King Louis for a fleet. Finally the king put a small group of French ships under John's command: the frigates *Alliance* and *Pallas,* the brig *Vengeance,* and the *Cerf, Monsieur,* and *Granville.* It wasn't the fleet John felt he deserved, but it was a command—in name, at least. The French ships sailed under French captains, who resented John's authority and ignored his orders.

Shortly after leaving France on June 19, 1779, the *Bonhomme Richard* and *Alliance* bumped each other, tangling their rigging and damaging both ships' masts. John believed that Captain Landais of the *Alliance* was at fault for refusing to acknowledge his flag signals. The French captain tried to break up the fleet by insisting that the *Richard* was to blame. To keep his command together, John decided to accept responsibility. He reluctantly dismissed his officer of the deck. The incident wasn't a good omen for the fleet's ability to work together.

John's ships captured the HMS *Union,* which was carrying a cargo of British army uniforms. Trying to be polite, John gave Captain Landais the honor of bringing in the *Union.* But that didn't improve their relationship. John still faced French resentment.

Refusing to give up, he sailed the *Bonhomme Richard* back to sea, forcing his fleet to follow. No matter how many times he had to prove his worth, John was determined that his men would esteem him enough to follow his command willingly.

6

"I Have Not Yet Begun to Fight"

In September John's *Bonhomme Richard* led the *Alliance, Pallas,* and *Vengeance* on a raid against the city of Leith, Scotland. Heavy winds prevented the squadron from landing, but its presence upset people. Scarborough Castle raised a red flag, signaling an enemy threat.

John also captured a ship whose pilot told him about a convoy of forty-one British ships. They were sailing down the northeast coast of England, carrying naval supplies. Surely such a prize would prove John's worth to Congress and bring him the American fleet he deserved!

The sloop *Countess of Scarborough* and the frigate HMS *Serapis* were escorting the convoy. John knew they would see Scarborough Castle's red flag when they sailed around Flamborough Head. This was a point of high cliffs jutting out into the sea. He hid his ships just around the point. As soon as the convoy appeared on September 23, John sailed forward.

The convoy drew back when the four ships appeared from behind the cliffs. The *Serapis* and *Scarborough* were clearly outgunned. But Captain Richard Pearson of the *Serapis* had to protect the convoy. At six o'clock in the evening, John raised his signal flags, telling his French ships to get in formation for battle. To his surprise, Captain Landais promptly deserted, sailing the *Alliance* away with the *Pallas* and the *Vengeance* right behind.

John wasn't willing to back down. As the sun set, he positioned his crew at their guns and on the top deck with grappling irons. He also sent seamen with grenades and muskets into the rigging, the way they'd drilled. In the dark before moonrise, Captain Pearson hailed the ship. Buying time to close in, John identified his ship as the *Princess Royal*. Pearson demanded to know where they were from.

Deciding they'd gotten as near as trickery would permit, John raised the American flag. He and

Pearson ran out their guns and fired on each other at almost the same moment. But the old, used cannons that John had bought failed him. The eighteen-pound cannonballs should have been his best weapon against the British warship. To make them as effective as possible, John had sent his best officers and crewmen to shoot them. But the old guns exploded when fired. The sailors were all killed or injured too badly to keep on fighting.

John pressed on, even though the *Serapis* had torn gaping holes out of the *Richard* and the *Scarborough* was firing at John's other side. He hoped to outrace the British ships and capture the convoy. Then Pearson fired a devastating broadside at close range.

Although his ship was in danger of sinking, John still refused to retreat. He abandoned his plan of out-running the warships. Instead, he used grappling irons to lock the *Serapis* and the *Bonhomme Richard* together. The *Scarborough* ceased fire, since any shots at the *Richard* now risked hitting the *Serapis.*

At eight o'clock, the moon rose, showing the damage to the *Richard* clearly. Pearson still had a little space between the two ships to run out his guns, so he kept firing. John called for more grappling irons to pull the ships closer together. He ordered his men to board the *Serapis,* but they were beaten back. Next he ordered his remaining deck guns to fire on the *Serapis*'s masts. And he had the men in the rigging throw grenades and shoot their muskets, chasing the British from the upper deck.

Then the French ships reappeared. The *Pallas* engaged the *Scarborough* and signaled to the *Alliance* for help, but Captain Landais had other plans. Ignoring his own countrymen, he sailed up to the *Serapis* and the *Richard*—and opened fire on the *Richard*! He hoped to sink John, then capture the damaged British frigate and claim the victory for himself. Landais fired three broadsides, killing men and flooding the lower deck. Unable to sink the *Richard*, Landais withdrew.

In the confusion, nobody was manning the deck guns. John took charge of three cannons himself, calling out the firing commands. The gun crew loaded and fired as the armed men in the rigging kept shooting. But the damage below decks was so severe that some of the junior officers panicked.

An officer named Henry Gardiner realized the *Richard* was sinking and tried to find a senior officer. Someone mistakenly told him that the lieutenant and captain had been killed. Gardiner thought he was the highest-ranking officer left alive. Crying "Quarter, quarter, our ship is sinking!" he ran to lower the flag.

When a ship hauled down its flag and asked for quarter, that meant it wanted to surrender.

John, still commanding his cannons, heard the cry. Furious, he ordered Gardiner shot. He had just fired his own pistols at the *Serapis,* so he threw one of the empty pistols at Gardiner, knocking him unconscious. But Pearson had also heard. He demanded to know if the *Richard* was surrendering.

Standing on the deck of a sinking flagship, betrayed by his allies, John stubbornly shouted his refusal. The earliest record of the event reports that he replied, "I have not yet thought of that, but I am determined to make you ask for quarter!" Lieutenant Richard Dale, serving with John on the *Richard,* recalls his captain answering, "I have not yet begun to fight!"

Heartened by their captain's determination, the men in the rigging increased their musket fire and the rain of grenades. They destroyed the deck guns on the *Serapis.* Then a well-aimed grenade hit some gunpowder bags. Fire erupted on deck and raced to the gun deck below. Smoke and flames forced the men out.

Captain Pearson knew that his ship could take no more. If he remained grappled to the *Richard* and sank it, he and his men would go down too. Pearson also knew that the convoy he'd been protecting had escaped to safety while the battle raged. He lowered his flag and asked for quarter. John said proudly that Pearson "came with his officers from the *Serapis* onto the *Bonhomme Richard* and presented me with his sword."

After he surrendered, Pearson got two surprises. First, John graciously returned his sword as a mark of esteem for a gallant opponent. Second, as John politely served Pearson a glass of wine in his cabin, the British captain realized the *Bonhomme Richard* was already sinking.

Before the *Richard* went down, John transferred his men, his prisoners, and his flag to the *Serapis* and sailed home. It was a worthy prize, though in terrible condition from the beating John had given it. Even though he'd failed to capture the convoy with its cargo, John was welcomed in France as the conquering hero of a great revolutionary navy.

Afterword: Universal Esteem

John's victories against British ships turned the tide in the sea war. King Louis XVI of France had already sent some troops to America. But he thought the French navy couldn't win against the British navy. John's raids on British ports and his success in scattering British warships proved that the British navy could be beaten.

King Louis honored John with the Order of Military Merit. He also gave John a beautiful sword. The king had it engraved to the man who defended the "Freedom of the Seas." And France sent more soldiers and ships to America to fight in critical battles. At Yorktown, Virginia, in 1781, the French fleet drove away British warships to support George Washington's victory.

John returned to America in 1781 also. Congress voted him thanks "for his bold and successful enterprises." They gave him the *America,* but the British surrendered before he could take command. The navy disbanded.

Longing to serve his adopted country any way he could, John urged Congress to create a full-time navy. He also recommended opening a school to train naval officers. He wrote, "In time of Peace, it is necessary to prepare, and be always prepared, for War by Sea." But Congress was busy establishing the United States government. They honored John by making him a commodore, but they couldn't see the need for a professional navy or a training school.

John was used to running up against people who ignored his recommendations. But he always refused to surrender, stubbornly repeating his ideas until someone listened. He kept on putting himself on the line to show how well his theories worked in action. When he was invited to Russia to lead a fleet, John seized the chance.

John got to work training the Russian sailors as soon as he arrived. They admired John and fought well under his command. He was made Rear Admiral Jones, but he still hoped to be called back to serve the United States. He left Russia in 1790 and traveled to France.

From Paris, John wrote to American friends. He reminded them of his success in the Continental navy and the Russian navy. He repeated his ideas about a naval training school. He asked for any government appointment at all, thinking that once he had a government position he could find support to start his school. John's determination wore down his opponents. In 1792 he was appointed commissioner to Algiers.

Before the news arrived, John complained of not feeling well. On the evening of July 18, 1792, forty-five-year-old John was alone in his Paris apartment. He collapsed face down on his bed and was found dead later that night. John was buried in a small cemetery for foreigners outside Paris. French Freemasons and officers attended his funeral to honor his memory.

It had always taken John a long time to convince people that his unconventional ideas had merit. It took Congress until 1798 to agree that the United States needed a full-time navy. Then, finally, in 1845, John's dream came true when Congress founded the United States Naval Academy in Annapolis, Maryland. To this day, the academy uses John as an example of brilliant problem-solving, strong leadership, and fearlessness in battle.

In 1905 President Theodore Roosevelt brought John's body home in honor to rest in the Naval Academy Chapel. The engraved sword from King Louis XVI of France is displayed beside him. Today the United States esteems the father of its navy with such deep respect that a Marine guard keeps eternal watch at his crypt.

Seafaring Terms

brig: see *warship*

broadside: cannon fire in which all the cannons on one side of a ship shoot at the same time

fleet: a group of warships under a single leader's command

frigate: see *warship*

grappling: using large iron hooks to lock an enemy ship against one's own. Grappling kept both ships from firing cannons. It also allowed sailors to board the enemy ship to fight hand to hand.

merchant ship: a ship built to carry goods for trading

mutiny: a violent rising up of sailors against their ship's captain

navigation: the science of determining a ship's position and plotting its course

rigging: the complex arrangement of ropes that supports a ship's masts and adjusts the sails

sloop: see *warship*

warship: a ship built to make war at sea. Warships were built strong enough to carry heavy cannons yet sleek enough for quick steering. In order of size, the warships that John Paul Jones commanded included:

sloop: a very small ship with triangular sails hung from one mast. Sloops carried ten to twenty cannons.

brig: a small ship with rectangular sails hung from two masts. Brigs carried fifteen to thirty cannons.

frigate: a fast, larger warship with rectangular sails hung from three masts. Frigates carried thirty to fifty cannons.

Selected Bibliography

Allen, Gardner W. *A Naval History of the American Revolution.* Williamstown, MA: Corner House Books, 1970.

Boudriot, Jean. *John Paul Jones and the* Bonhomme Richard. Translated by David H. Roberts. Annapolis, MD: Naval Institute Press, 1987.

Gilkerson, William. *The Ships of John Paul Jones.* Annapolis, MD: Naval Institute Press, 1987.

Lorenz, Lincoln. *John Paul Jones, Fighter for Freedom and Glory.* Annapolis, MD: U. S. Naval Institute, 1943.

Mackenzie, Alexander Slidell. *The Life of John Paul Jones.* Boston: Hilliard, Gray and Company, 1841.

Morison, Samuel Eliot. *John Paul Jones: A Sailor's Biography.* Boston: Little, Brown, 1959.

Index

Alfred, 27–30, 37–38
Alliance, 48, 51, 53

Barbados, 13–15, 19
Benson, Robert, 12
Betsy, 21–22
Bonhomme Richard, 46–50, 52–56
brig, 10, 12, 17, 19
broadside, 30, 52, 53
Burgoyne, John, 41

cannon, 27–28, 36–37, 48, 52–55
capturing ships, 31–33, 37–38, 49, 53, 56
colonies, American, 9, 14–15, 19, 25–26
Congress, 25–27, 33, 35, 37, 40, 42, 46, 50, 57, 59
Craik, Mr., 9, 10, 21

Dale, Richard, 55
Dandridge, Dorothea, 26
discipline, 13, 19–20, 22, 33, 40–41

fleet, 8, 44, 46
Franklin, Benjamin, 41, 46
Freemasons, 20, 26, 58
Friendship, 10, 12–13, 43
frigate, 33, 38, 40, 45, 48, 53

Gardiner, Henry, 53–55
grappling, 36, 48, 51–52, 55

Hancock, John, 40
Henry, Patrick, 26
Hewes, Joseph, 26, 27
HMS *Drake,* 45
HMS *Glasgow,* 28–30
HMS *Mellish,* 37–38
HMS *Serapis,* 51–56
Hopkins, Eset, 28, 30

Jamaica, 16
Jefferson, Thomas, 26
John (brig), 17, 19
John (merchant ship), 37–38
Jones, John Paul: appearance of, 7, 21; as apprentice, 10–15; buys land, 21; as captain in navy, 31, 33, 40; captures enemy ships, 31–33, 38, 49, 56; childhood, 7–15; desire for esteem, 15, 17, 20–21, 24, 26, 31, 41–42; disliked by his crews, 19, 22, 40–41; education, 8, 10; as father of the navy, 59; as fleet commander, 48–56; as lieutenant in navy, 27–28; love of America, 14–15; as master of ships, 18–22; moves to Virginia, 24–25; murder charges, 20–24; name change, 24; after Revolutionary War, 57–59; unusual ideas of, 33–37, 42, 44–45, 59

knots, 9, 10

Landais, Captain, 48, 51, 53
life at sea, 12–13, 40–41
Louis XVI, king of France, 41, 46, 48, 57, 59

Maxwell, Mungo, 19–21
merchant ship, 27, 30, 37, 46
mutiny, 22–24

naval warfare, 25–34, 36–38, 51–56
navigation, 15, 17
navy, British, 10, 27, 37, 42, 44–46, 57
navy, Continental, 26–27, 31, 34, 57–58

Paul, Elizabeth (sister), 8
Paul, Janet (sister), 8
Paul, John Junior. *See* Jones, John Paul
Paul, John Senior (father), 8–10, 17
Paul, Mary Ann (sister), 8
Paul, William (brother), 9, 14, 20, 24
Pearson, Richard, 51, 55–56
Providence, 30–33

raid, 42–45, 50, 57
Ranger, 40–46
Revolutionary War, 26, 44
rigging, 10, 13, 37, 48, 53, 55
Ringleader, 22
River Nith, 7, 8, 12, 19

Roosevelt, Theodore, 59

Saltonstall, Dudley, 27–28, 31, 37
Scotland, 7, 8, 14, 20, 28, 50
Selkirk, Earl of, 45
Seven Years' War, 13
slavery, 15–16
sloop, 30–33, 40, 46

taxes, 25
Tobago, 19, 21–24
training, 27–30, 35, 37, 48, 57–59

uniforms, 35, 37, 38, 49
U. S. Naval Academy, 59

Virginia, 9, 14, 16, 24

warship, 7, 26–31, 34, 36, 42, 44, 46, 48, 57
Washington, George, 15, 26, 38, 57
West Indies, 16, 19, 21
Whitehaven, England, 10, 43–44

Younger's Shipping Company, 10, 15

About the Authors

Elaine Marie Alphin loves to discover the fascinating stories behind the people and things that changed history. She has written more than twenty books for young readers, including *Davy Crockett, Germ Hunter, Telephones, Toasters,* and *Vacuum Cleaners.* Her award-winning fiction includes *Ghost Soldier,* which was nominated for the 2002 Edgar Allan Poe Award in the Best Juvenile Mystery category and won the 2002 Society of Midland Authors Award for Children's Fiction, and her latest mystery, *Picture Perfect.* Readers can learn more about Ms. Alphin's books at <http://www.elainemariealphin.com>.

Arthur B. Alphin loves history, especially military history. He enlisted in the U.S. Army and went on to graduate from the U.S. Military Academy at West Point as a tank officer and weapons engineer. He earned his M.A. from Rice University and taught military history and technology at both Rice and West Point. Colonel Alphin has won the Abrams Award for his technical and historical writing for adults. *I Have Not Yet Begun to Fight* is his first book for young readers. But he had such a good time collaborating with his wife to write history for young people that he has already written a biography of Dwight D. Eisenhower with her and has more ideas for future works.

About the Illustrator

Paul Casale is an award-winning fine artist and illustrator who often exhibits his work in New York City. Along with painting portraits and landscapes, he has created artwork for many children's books. He expecially enjoys combining traditional art techniques with modern subjects. Casale lives in Cranford, New Jersey.